Night Highway

Night Highway

Barbara Koons

*For Jenny,
with best wishes —
Barbara Koons Jan 10 2007*

Cloudbank Books
Corvallis, Oregon

© 2004 by Barbara Koons. All rights reserved.

This book, or any part thereof, may not be reproduced by any means, written or mechanical, or be programmed into any electronic retrieval or information storage system, without express written permission from the publisher, except for short passages for purpose of review.

First Edition

Library of Congress Cataloging in Publication Data

Barbara Koons, 1935 -
Night Highway

ISBN: 0-9665018-7-X

Cloudbank Books
P.O. Box 610
Corvallis, OR 97339-0610
Cloudbank Books is an imprint of

Bedbug Press
P.O. Box 39
Brownsville, OR 97327

Cover art by Judith Parenio
Cover design and book design by M'Liss Runyon
Cloudbank Books logo is a carving by Julie Hagan Bloch from *Haunting Us With His Love* by David Samuel Bloch.
Text set in Bookman
Printed at Friesens, Altona, Manitoba, Canada

*For my children,
in loving memory of my parents.*

CONTENTS

I

Train Town Blues	3
Silk	5
Apron Strings	7
Flight School	8
Westbound	9
Three Children At The Shore	11
Souvenir	13
Getting It All Together	15
The Clock-maker's Daughter	17
Handing Down The Recipe	19
Granddaughter	20
September	21

II

Why We Cry At Weddings	25
Insomniac Hitchhiker	26
Night Watch	27
Ladies' Lunch At The Shedd Aquarium	28
Cocktail Hour With Barbie and Ken	29
Stained Glass	30
Evening In Paris	31
Fire In Winter	33
Wedding Ghost	34
Glass Flowers	36
Traveling With Dr. Death	38
On The Night Highway	41
Dove Call	42

III

New Moon Rising	47
Sky Harbor	48
Casa Rural	50
Cooking With A Cuban Jazz Drum Solo	52
Hide And Seek	54
The Robin's Egg	55
The Window	56
White Wake	57
Widow's Love Song	59
Monarch	60

IV

Exposing The Negative	65
Raspberry Gathering	67
Celebrating Her 80th	69
Geraniums	70
The Gift	71
Silent Movie	72
Homecoming	73
There's This About Loss	74
A Gardener's Guide To The Cosmos	75
Moon Shining Through Trees	76
The Clearing	77
Tree House	78

*"It is not that the darkness
must be there, but that it sometimes is."*

—Linda Gregg

I

TRAIN TOWN BLUES
Mansfield, Ohio, 1953

Where trains never stop,
hollyhocks and tall grasses
line backyard fences,
and poplar trees shuffle leaves
soft as an old deck of cards.

Steel mill volcanos spill
fountains of fireworks
on the horizon,
where winter sky glows
orange as the 4th of July.

Iron lions track a grid
rigid as a teacher's ruler,
divide north from south,
thunder under day and night,
rumble through sleep.

Like bookends, the gravestones
hold us together,
while the country club dances
on the only lawn in town
where there are no dandelions.

On wooden porches,
whisky and gin,
brown-bagged neat.
Queasy stomachs
seek respite in blue glass
Alka Seltzer bottles.

In the nature museum
up the stone stairs
above the picture show,
stuffed pheasants molt.
Pickled in yellowing brine,
dead babies float in clouded jars.

Baby pigs, baby lambs,
what's the difference
between the two?

Between the two garages,
that damp tunnel
between boys and girls,
what's the difference?

All are smooth
mushrooms, cool and pale,
toe bones in the shoe store
X-ray. All bones glow
the same in the dark.

Every Easter, new black patent shoes.
Every September, a blue plaid dress.

Outside the high school,
under the abandoned roller coaster,
behind the burned-out skating rink,
Camel cigarettes flare. In closets,
girls stuff their bras with Kleenex.

Downtown at the five and dime
cheap underwear, fake leather belts,
new cardboard suitcases,
line up in rows, waiting.

On both sides of the tracks
train music
whistles seduction,
and all over town,

high tangles of summer
jump fences,
creep into sleep
through all the unlocked doors.

SILK

Melon hue of evening sky
when April sun has bartered
with an all-day rain, and won
the right to lilac fire:
your first formal gown

not home-sewn, bought
from the gaunt spinster who sold
dreams off racks
to high school girls
above a record shop.

You did not hear
"Your Cheatin' Heart's"
warning tones
drift up the wooden stairs.
Your ears were tuned to "Lohengrin"

when, like a gilded peach, silk
caressed your skin, soft as breath,
warm as your own flesh, and his,
the boy you danced with
and whose name you thought
you'd long forgotten,
folded away with the dress.
And then April

rain dissolves years,
the trunk falls open,
silk slides through memory
like a familiar voice.

I lean against the rough oak frame
of my open kitchen door, and feel
his arms around me.

I rest my cheek on glass, cool
and smooth as silk, the tie
he borrowed from his dad.

From the blue
echo of a saxophone,
old songs rise like honey,
slow and gold as the moon,
and with my own pulse humming
like a muffled drum,
I close my eyes,
raise my arms,
and dance.

APRON STRINGS

Is cutting an art
best mastered by sons,
honed by fathers, who know
the fastest way through a knot is a slash?

I cannot teach my daughter
the silver skill of slicing
fish from a hook, dropping scales
like buttons from a worn-out shirt.

From me, she learns
the art of weaving
one thread into another.
When a strand is cut we slide
a new one through the needle's eye.

"Watch me," says the father, "watch me."

I say to my daughter,
"Take my hand."

When my son inherits his father's watch,
my daughter will carry, deep in her hands
the bones of my fingers,

lumpy as clothespins, but nimble,
still able to fasten
new lives onto the line.

FLIGHT SCHOOL

Too young for cars,
too cool for swings and slides,
young teens wheel up the hill on bikes,
calling out to each other,
their voices high and clear
as the cries of wild geese.

Inside the chain link fence
at the grade school playground,
they scuff torn sneakers in dust,
sensing an inner pull—

when to stay and when to go,
how to travel unknown skies
without maps, to find their own way—

they drop their bikes,
swing out beyond the fence
and in again on rusty chains,
their weight shaking the creaking frame,
over and over returning them
to center point,
and the rush of wind beneath.

WESTBOUND

"Buy me a ticket on the last train home tonight."
— Al Stewart,
"Time Passages"

Whenever a train rolls its old song
through my sleep, the long blue call
wraps around me and I go along,
holding my father's hand again,
walking out the railroad tracks
behind the roller skating rink, beyond
the purple thump and roll
of the old pipe organ; beyond

the boarded and fallen amusement park,
the roller coaster that finally collapsed,
falling in on itself.
A matchstick tower. A dinosaur skeleton.
I'm in the museum of the mind. It's the night

the Congregational Church burns down, and Father
snatches me from bed, runs with me
just in time to see the steeple fall. Steam hisses
from the huge black engine, and we're running
to jump the trestle, running from plunging

iron, rumble, rubble, smoke;
my father's white handkerchief
shields my eyes from cinders,
and then we're waving to the brakeman,
riding the rattling caboose,
following the train home. In truth,

the train is following me. I don't look back,
dare not, must not,
see it gaining on me. And Father,
I am coming home tonight,
before dark, before the scaffolding falls
in a sparking red arc, before the westbound
leaves the station and you become the brakeman,
waving me down the track.

THREE CHILDREN AT THE SHORE

We clatter along the hollow boards
in the weathered bathhouse every summer,
dashing straight for sun and water,
running the wide expanse of coast
on Lake Erie's Cedar Point, where the blue
sky floats balloons for me, the child

of parents who also are children
for a single day each year. The board-
walk leads us to a row of blue
painted tables, where we eat summer
sausage with mustard by the coast
of cresting waves, washed down with watery

pink lemonade. My mouth still waters
for coney dogs, when I see children
playing on a beach. I coast
the wind of memory, and board
once more the carousel of summer.
I ride a hand-carved horse with blue

glass eyes. The music clangs bright blue,
just slightly out of tune. Water
carries the sound into summer
sky, and round and round I go,
forever a child, high on board
the rattling track the roller coaster

rocks along until it coasts,
creaking, to halt beside the blue-
roofed candy stand. We buy cardboard
boxes filled with stale salt-water
taffy to take home, for the child
in each of us who wishes for summer

to last forever. Our one-day summer
vacation ends where it began, the coast
of Sandusky Bay, where three children
with sun-pink skin wait for the blue
ferry boat to bear them over the water.
Until it docks, there are three kids aboard.

At the board pier, one child and two adults
step off, to coast home in the summer night,
leaving behind water, blue sky, and sun.

SOUVENIR

My father caged paper lions
with matchstick bars;
folded, pasted, painted, strung
a toothpick trapeze from a fishing line;
and The Greatest Show On Earth
paraded across our dining-room floor
into a tablecloth tent,
marching to brass razz-ma-tazz
only we could hear.

Our small ringmaster
in his red-crayon jacket
eventually disappeared
into the vacuum cleaner,
along with several monkeys and a clown.
Our elephants were overcome
by the roaring wind of its maw,
forgotten

until today, with my own children,
seated in a steel arena
higher than a trapeze glides—

Far below, a ringmaster
with my father's eyes
snaps a whip-crack recognition.

My cardboard circus shimmers
in white-striped zebra light,
flashing me back,
back into a dusty tent
billowing luminous as a balloon,

with tigers bursting red
through orange paper fire;
drums, trumpets, dancing dogs,
popcorn, peanuts, souvenirs—

The ringmaster bows
with my father's smile, tells me,

"Take your circus home with you,
tucked into a secret pocket.
Slide your childhood tongue around it.
Taste glitter, grit and straw.
It's your chameleon, green and fleeting;
your pink and peacock feather bird,
singing in a yellow wind,
a purple pasteboard sky."

GETTING IT ALL TOGETHER

I want to take it all along—
apples falling in the orchard,
grapes ripening sweet and purple
in an August night, begonias
opening white wax petals, snow
melting so quickly in sunlight,
the summer days of my children,
whose short childhoods I wasted;
my ex-husband, the man whose name I kept
years after he had strayed.
I see hollyhock dolls floating away,
unencumbered by possessions,
like ice show girls who drift along
with no apparent legs or feet,
and know I've lived my life all wrong.
I always pack the wrong clothing
for every trip, and toss away
prize-winning lottery stubs.
Trying to go by all the rules
I learned from Hollywood scripts,
the things I thought I'd need still spill
out of my old scrapbooks.
Matches, sugar packets, candy
wrappers, gum—I had those pages
stocked like a pharaoh's tomb,
papered with unlined faces.
I used to dream about the test
that I was unprepared to take—
these days my nightmares
center on planes departing without me,
while I endlessly sort my belongings.
I must fold and pack the scent of roses

rising in moonlight
beneath our bedroom window
in the first small house we owned.
I'll take the house, too—

detach the downspouts,
buckle in the walls like cardboard.
It will expand again into rooms
when I unfold the roof.
The children will bounce from their beds,
laughing; their father will be there
at the breakfast table,
and all our lost cats and dogs
will be lined up,
just outside the kitchen door.

THE CLOCK-MAKER'S DAUGHTER

Beyond the counter where I stand,
the door into the workroom frames
her portrait like a small Renoir—
her face, the focal point of light,
eyes steady blue beneath the blond
hair falling smooth upon a white
blouse, its collar edged in lace.
Perched on a stool, she leans toward
her father's hands, her own hands clasped.
She's tucked one foot beneath her;
the other, in a pink sock, swings free.

I have brought in the antique clock
from my grandfather's pharmacy.
It lies before the clock-maker,
its hands and face removed. I watch
the child's eyes follow her father's hands
as he probes into brass and steel.
The image of the two of them,
intent among the rosewood tones
and shadows of mahogany,
turns in my mind, an old key
unlocking a familiar door—

where Grandfather halves a tulip bulb
to show me how the flower hides,
it isn't there when parchment
layers fall away. My clock
begins its slow tick-tock,
blending into other clocks,
like water running slow as melting snow.
I see the suns and moons revolve
in unison, and understand

the click of memory that stops
within another time and place

and then swings on. I am
still there, in the pharmacy,
with its tall rows of wooden drawers,
medicinal odors of peppermint,
camphor, cloves, cod-liver oil—
still the child who sits
beside her grandfather at work,
perched on a stool, breathing in
the scents of his mysterious trade—

and at the same time, I am here,
part of today, in this small shop
where my memory swings, like her foot,
back and forth, back and forth.

HANDING DOWN THE RECIPE

My kitchen distills aromas more potent
than Grandmother's cinnamon and vanilla.
I drink summer mornings with a thirst
unquenched in childhood, when we gathered
wild elderberries for pies and jam,
pulling their clusters from supple stems
like beads from green silk threads.

I hadn't yet learned what I know now.
Old wood hardens, becomes close-grained.
Mature fruit ferments into brew
intoxicating as the power
Grandmother knew and kept secret:
She could taste
invisible sips of the future.

Her luck at cards was uncanny.
She knew when snow would come.
She marked her February destiny
on her calendar, ink-blacked
the square of her death, leaving us
an heirloom enigmatic as an empty mirror.

Her pulse rises in my veins,
fills the crystal stem of memory
with ink that links our lives.
Her pen is in my hand, brittle
as an old twig, poised, waiting
for her gnarled script
to flow across the page,

tracing old recipes, pouring out
a purple rush for me to drink
on a winter night, a liqueur
pungent, wild, and tart as elderberry wine.

GRANDDAUGHTER

Daughter of my daughter,
you crawl across the floor
to the same table
my grandmother used
to roll out cookies
like these I'm making now, for you,

with her recipe and utensils
handed down to me. From her kitchen
above Grandfather's pharmacy
came crisp sugared angels,
Christmas trees and bells,
hearts and stars.
This morning, light as your hair
rising in wisps of sunlight,

milkweed smoke floats
in Grandfather's glass humidor
on the shelf above my stove.
Beside it chimes his clock,
turning time in steady rhythm.
Like sparks from his cigar,
red paper arrows mark the hours

the streetcar stopped
in front of his shop
on its run through my childhood.
Today, as you bang on her tin baking tray
with the same wooden spoon Grandmother used
to stir her galaxy of stars,
the streetcar stops in my kitchen,
while our lives, without pause, clang by.

SEPTEMBER

A softening of light, the scent of wheat,
and nectar-laden August air
distills into September's chardonnay.
I hear the song wild finches sing,
the rasp of insects in corn stalks
in fields now burnished bronze with goldenrod,

and remember the feel of denim, clean
against my skin, the warmth of sun
through open windows in my old grade school.
I think I hear a cast-iron bell, and in its spell
I'm sure if I walk down a dusty road
beyond the pavement's end, and wait
beside a fence where sunflowers grow,
a yellow bus will come for me.

II

WHY WE CRY AT WEDDINGS

Because

>on those distant summer afternoons
when we stood, sweating
before God and Company,
vowing aloud promises
whispered in back seats
fragrant with wheat fields
and Queen Anne's lace,

No one warned us

>of promises broken, crushed
like bodies of small animals
along the road;

And because

>even now, with heads bowed
in other summer churches,
we are gathered, dearly beloved,
to watch our own children
depart on roads of their own.
Standing with folded hands,
helpless as wheat field virgins,

We are unable to foretell

>whose dreams will survive
and whose will rot,
like fur and feathers
in the dust.

INSOMNIAC HITCHHIKER

Wandering the uncertain berm
between here and gone, I balance
on the edge of slumber,
a stranger in my own dreams.

Uninvited sounds
ramble in and out the window,
brazen as party-crashers, bringing along
their dogs and cats. Within the walls
mice whisper secrets. Out on the highway

semis rumble. The night bus passes,
gearing into high, carrying the hopeful
and the bereaved. So well I know
the contents of their baggage,
I might have packed it myself.

Finally, all the humming tires roll
beyond the rim of my awareness,
leaving me behind,
a flipped cigarette
wheeling into oblivion.

NIGHT WATCH

You and I, and our fantasies.
Every night the same four strangers
board a night-boat going nowhere,
adrift among shadows, tossing
on pillows with no cool side.

We stare into the dark,
watch the silver
backing the mirror
crackle and peel,
leaving blank patches
where our eyes should be.

Pull up some chairs.
We'll open the curtains,
turn on the moon.
We can all play bridge,
or perhaps, charades.

LADIES' LUNCH AT THE SHEDD AQUARIUM, CHICAGO

Among the fish,
women gather to be fed,
trailing pastel chiffon
through a perfumed sea,
their mouths opening and closing
persistently as gills.

Life is served, and it is good;
if it were not, would they admit it?
Not likely, not in this transparent bowl.
They know how to leave space
between each other on every level.

On the rolling waves of their voices
one perfect round O after another
bubbles to the surface
as they circle the shining rim,
devouring gossip, careful not to touch
each other, or the glass walls
insulating them from the world.

COCKTAIL HOUR WITH BARBIE AND KEN

The man who loomed so large
grows smaller and smaller,
a postage stamp hero
flatter than a Sunday comic.

Barbie, what did you see in him?
Couldn't you tell
he was paper, so thin
you could cut him
with a sigh? Remember

how he used to undress you,
pose the two of you naked
after the children were asleep?
Have you forgotten
how he made your stiff joints squeak?

Those were the nights you drank
Grant's Stand Fast Scotch,
watched "Gunsmoke,"
ate pizza in bed.

Ah, Barbie,
you never suspected
both of you were plastic.
You just assumed you'd live
happily ever after.

Every time a baby came
he brought you a dozen roses.

After the third, you said,
"Forget the flowers.
Just bring a bottle of Grant's."

STAINED GLASS

Rain for breakfast,
damp shoes, wet wool, smoke,
an old stone fireplace—

As if opened by rain, a glass lotus
glows pale yellow, an opaque shell
reflecting the Pacific,
blurring the Big Sur landscape
rolling green with silver.

An ad for a country inn,
but you and I could be the ones who sit
beside the intricate window

inhaling the spray of citrus
while we separate pink grapefruit,
making small talk,
as if life itself could be divided
so neatly into sections. Inside, outside.

Rain washes down the striped awning,
I pour steaming water over jasmine tea.

Soon, each of us will try
to drown all memory of this moment,
hoping to clear to innocence,
a streaked sky-light opening,
unfurling clear blue.

But none of this has happened yet.
Only the rain, and the yearning,
the leaded stems unbending.

EVENING IN PARIS

With gin buzzing in my ears
like a persistent mosquito,
the dark hot room
where I slept as a child
seems so much smaller
five strides cross it,

span years. In my mind
my wedding gown
still shimmers on the closet door,
my ticket out of town.

Sweating beside me
in the sagging bed,
my husband sprawls, snoring;
dreaming, I suppose, of his lover.

All day we traveled
toward the past, and now
I'm the only one awake
in this high school moon night

blue as the glass
perfume vial still lying
on my dressing table,
its breath of wilted violets

limp as the curtains
in the humid darkness.
Evening In Paris.
A man I did not marry
dances with his wife.

I give up on sleep,
light a cigarette.
Like the first hot flash
of lightning, the match
flares in the mirror,
illuminates another face
I no longer remember.

FIRE IN WINTER

Hope. It's a joke, a fake
birthday candle, re-kindling
breath after breath. Stubborn
as a January dandelion,

it blazes on the frozen lawn.
I put it out. It flares again,
forsythia's yellow flame
exploding in too-early sun.

Daffodil fires glow
beyond every window,
choirs of children
bearing lighted candles
that will not be extinguished
no matter how strong the wind
or raw the rain that blows
damp into every crevice.

Matters have taken me
into their hands.
Flaming flowers ring my fingers.

Five candles burn, ten candles,
my hands are candelabra.
Bracelets of fire slide up my arms.

I admire their glitter, watch while sparks
wrap orange silk around my shoulders.
Beyond pain, I wonder

What will remain?
Bones? A gold ring?
Or one eye, glowing, red,
a smoldering coal?

WEDDING GHOST

Packed away like my favorite doll,
dressed in her lavish trousseau,
my wedding gown lies folded in my attic.
Every day was wedding day
for that small bride who stood alone,
perpetually poised
on the threshold of her future.

I never saw a groom doll
except on top of a wedding cake,
a hollow plastic statue
wedded to a tiny bride,
an accessory to virginity.
I can't remember
when I abandoned my doll,
closed her big soft eyes.
I don't know why

I keep my gown and veil,
pearls and sequins shimmering
like fireflies in a jar;
shriveled roses tied with silver ribbon;
lacy lingerie, pristine
as an heirloom christening gown.

I should give it all away
to a vintage clothing shop,
cut up the silk for pillows,
wear the damned thing on Halloween.

Instead I drag an empty shroud,
all that's left of my marriage,
along with me from house to house,

and I wonder when and where,
on whose doorstep
will it finally reappear,

this phantom of a former life I've buried
in a sealed box lined in satin,
white and silent
as the coffin of a child.

GLASS FLOWERS

A spring ice storm, then sun
warms floral carpet.
My life has become my grandmother's
Victorian glass paperweight,
I am trapped
in its shining prism.

I want out. I can't stand
the glass flowers,
their saccharine perfume
suffocates me.

Ice glazes pink tulips,
turns hyacinths into blue grapes.
Jonquils glisten like lemons
among green glass leaves.

I snap off
all the frozen buds,
cold and hard as marbles:

He loves me, he loves
me not, he loves me,
loves me, loves me not.

Each water droplet sliding
the length of its crystal stem
strengthens my glittering cage.

I have no air. My breath
congeals. I must smash
the sky, hurl boulders
until the clear dome shatters,
crashes down in splinters of sleet.

I pick up rage like a stone,
claw the earth with my fingers
for pebbles, gravel, sand—

With bare feet, I crush
petals and leaves into slivers.
Paying no heed to Haviland roses,
sweeping smashed Waterford under the rug,

I explode from the dome
in a wild burst of lightning,
a thunderous storm of my own.

TRAVELING WITH DR. DEATH

"I think of myself as Death, sometimes. In
a scarlet shroud, floating through the night.
I'm so beautiful then. And sad.
And hungry to make the whole world happy,
by taking them out into the night, away from all trouble,
all unhappiness."
         — James M. Cain, *Double Indemnity*

I've bought the ticket now,
I'm on the train we're all aboard.

A nurse
younger than I ever was
checks my baggage.
Her white cap bobs,
gives me motion sickness
when she inserts her silver needles.

I float away,
a dandelion puff,
reappear as breath
on a cold day.
I hear bells,
inhale scented air.
Crossings speed by,
red lights flash,

the train
thunders on,
pounding, blowing, spewing
bits of cinder. Walls revolve,
velvet fingers stroke
tubing down my throat.

Venom bubbles up
bitter as spoiled olives,
their centers gone rancid.

When the porter comes,
I order a martini.
He serves it frozen solid.

My parched lips can't suck it
up the straw. I lick
a lemon stick. No juice flows.
I inhale candy cigarettes,
lipstick-tipped;
the world tilts.

Under my bed, the night
light crawls beneath the door,
an evil beetle.
A nurse enters,
squashes it. Does she
wear a mask
or a beard?

Her electric hair
glows like a gas flame.
She rinses it
in Little Boy Blue.
It crackles with static
out of sync with the monitor
jump-starting my heart.

Her aura accelerates
my inner rhythm. There is no

stopping now. Rubber hoses
snake around me tight as pythons.
My eyes no longer focus,
clocks wear two faces,
gold-rimmed pain embraces me,
blood tulips burst into bloom.

I unfurl a thin red kite, float
higher and higher, let go
my tether. Weightless,

I rise above gravity.
Colors dim, sound fades,
air evaporates into a void,
blackness consumes my shadow—

I am light.

ON THE NIGHT HIGHWAY

At midnight, winter sky
looses its summer transparency
in vapor trails riding
either side of the moon,

as if a lone vehicle has rolled
on giant wheels
across a vast black field.

The air is so still
I can hear silent bells
rusting in deserted churches,
their naves empty
of all salvation.

Sometimes
I drive all night
just because
I don't want to sleep alone,

trying to understand loss,
the hour never found
on the face of every clock.

DOVE CALL

Your soft voice through the open door
calls me beyond the shining spill
lawn sprinklers pour from cut grass bowls
into summer evenings years and miles away,
where hide-and-seek and sweet grape dusk
and lily-scented shadows reign.

I scramble allee-allee-oxen-free,
barefoot, breathless, up wooden stairs
to a porch swing creaking a cricket song,
the chill silver of the ice cream bell,
streetlamps lighting, fire-flies glow—

Dove, I hear you, but I'm not coming home.

III

NEW MOON RISING

On the mirror of my dark side
I travel alone
over empty sea.

Skating over midnight ice
on a single shining blade,
a silver crescent.

I am a wind-blown
willow leaf floating the blue
sky river of peace.

Pear tree flowers, pale
in moonlight, moon-white fragrance
blossoms in night sky.

Star meadow shines on
crickets singing under pines.
Mine are silent dreams.

Firefly candles
glow in grass, champagne bubbles
rise in crystal stems,

Cardinals' red songs break
night's black glass. Rain spills
over into morning light.

Like the waning moon,
I travel light, float away
in an open boat.

Fresh from a shower, I come
to you, a wild rose
moist and sweet-scented with dew.

SKY HARBOR

Tonight, I believe in magic
Arabian nights—I'm flying
a carpet of stars as I leave
your city in light snow.
The swift take-off into low sky
becomes a dive into the Black Sea,
and I swim in slow motion
up from Arctic depths,
to surface on a tropical shore.
I catch my breath, I am floating

weightless over an ocean vista,
a trompe l'oeil too real to disbelieve.
I hover over fluid air,
long shallow tidal pools of sun,
still water shoals and bays, and mauve
sand bars. A massive rise of iris dunes
with silver sea grass bending in wind
silhouettes against deepening night.

I have left behind with you
the green geography I once knew,
and found the foreign landscapes mapped
in my old grade-school books.

The Easter-colored continents
float by now, they are Persian silk
and Chinese jade. I could accept
in this mirage a shining mosque,
the song of camel bells at dusk.
In this oasis, water is silver
reflected in sky, and now

the stars, the same as where you are
in snow. On an interstellar course
I give myself to flight
as if I am now a great, swift gull,
and you will be there to meet me
when I glide down into Earth's port
in a smooth sky harbor landing.

CASA RURAL

Thank you for your postcard
from Costa Rica. I can see
that your paper rain cottage may be
one of a few places remaining
where only poetry can
explain all the green,

where tranquility blooms
so deep in all seasons
cows lie down and meditate
in the front yard, where lava rocks float
like islands in herbal mist
so thick it carries the taste of time
unwinding into rain-forest shadows.

Was it you who left
the wooden ladder stacked
haphazard
against a slender tree?

I see you've gone
without closing the door,
although someone else has
boarded the windows
over-looking the verdant sea of ferns,
primordial ocean, and coral shells
opening souls to sky

on sand where sun
bleaches bones,
where too many moons
explode into clouds,
where white foam gathers
speed and thunder; and again
the rain, the never-ending

waterfall, drenching
tropical afternoons,

and it doesn't matter how many
lifetimes go by
listening to rain
on the tin roof.
It leaks, but never
mind the slow corrosion.

Here, there's no need to
plant roses, or even grass.
It all outgrows
the boundaries our minds set,
and it isn't necessary
to understand, just welcome

all those centuries
where there are no doors
that do not open
into summer gardens,
where we may dance
through long, slow, musical nights;

where both of us can breathe
under water.

COOKING WITH A CUBAN JAZZ DRUM SOLO

stage lights dim
every shining
silver point
gas flame blue

heat rising   beating begins
dark red
velvet feathers   sound
hovering

curtains part
flamingo!   pink
ocean rolls   hot
tropical froth   hurricane

wind drops
coconuts   thunder
rum silk
sugar cane   pineapple

mango mouths
caress   orchids
conch shell   ear
drums blare, skin bare,
hands, feet pumping
equatorial pulse   pure

orgasmic   copper
cymbals slice
avocado
butter yellow   flesh
inside ripe

seed bursts
open   palms
rustle fronds

warm wind floats
over water   still
that long cool
beating ripple
meringue smooth   half-moon
fingers delicate
apricot dawn

HIDE AND SEEK

Have you noticed
how the sun moves buildings—
slowly, inexorably, their shadows
trade places with those of the trees?

And have you noticed
how the shadows of falling leaves,
traveling the same channel of light,
always win the race to the earth?

Do you understand your life
will eventually turn into lace,
becoming more shadow than substance,
a thread connecting what was with what is?

And do you understand
how to read a map, to untangle
your own network of roads—
that somewhere within that skein

a black dot hides at the end of a line,
an empty space waiting for your shadow
to appear and then vanish,
sliding like the sun into sea?

THE ROBIN'S EGG

In soft grass underneath the pine
the egg is perfect, smooth and dry—
intact, uncracked, silent, still,
pale blue as Easter morning sky.
Hidden inside: clear morning songs,
a quick-cocked head, bright black eyes,
a jaunty bounce across the lawn,
lullabies crooned in evening dusk.
Like my own child's first child, the bird
inside, all wrapped in newborn blue—
that tender, terrible hue
of yarn, shawl, shroud—

Daughter, I bring this egg to you:
another life we never knew.

THE WINDOW

Every night, my father asks to be taken
to the window, where his reflection
gazes in at us from sky,

cold stars, Northern lights,
frost on stubble fields,
the apple tree—

At the end of his life,
he still loves apples,
which he no longer can pare,
core, or eat without help—

Years ago, he painted apples
spilling from a blue Delft bowl.
Red skin, white flesh, and deeper,
cider's amber gleam through glass—

I wish he could pour himself,
raw and clean,
into an old tin cup:

Glass, apples, shining reflection,
the flat metallic taste of tin,
rust, stem, seed—

Simply pass like lamplight
through to the other side,

as easily, painlessly
as wind and rain

evaporate, disappear,
become transparent air.

WHITE WAKE

On the summer morning
we buried my father,
we followed the hearse
past white farm houses,
chickens and picket fences.
Our wheels churned
a chalk dust wake
from the gravel road.
It settled on our faces
fine as a veil
at the country church
in a field
of wind-tossed dandelion puffs
airy as my father's bald fringe
on the satin pillow in the casket
where his body lay.

Through all the years
I knew him, my father
never left Ohio,
except to travel
on the Mississippi River.
Settling into his old arm chair,
hunkered down
like a turtle in mud,
he probed the flowing water,
exploring every cove and rapid
with Mark Twain as his guide.

Those nights, I suppose
he must have imagined
he was a rogue, a riverboat gambler,
with a full house in one hand
and a mint julep
in the other.

Days, we watched him
fulfill the visions
of his artist's eye. He painted
a yellow circus tent
beneath a bright red sky,
a forest of blue trees
shadowed mauve at dusk.

When he retired we gave him
a cruise on the Delta Queen—
Cincinnati to New Orleans.
He told us the Mississippi
was exactly as he imagined. "But,"
he confided to me, "there was no mint.
The bartender couldn't
make a mint julep for me."

At the cemetery
we crushed wild mint under our feet
walking across the field
where we parked the car.
Its green scent rose
light as fine spray,
lingered in the hushed
cool hollow of the church.

I closed my eyes, tried not to breathe
the sweetness my father was denied.

I bowed my head,
tasted the river,
and let my father disappear
on the wide white wake
of a paddlewheel steamer,
sipping a mint julep and holding four aces,
gliding into his own red sky.

WIDOW'S LOVE SONG

In the yellow house
where she came as a bride,
my mother wears my father's clothes,
ignores the mouse gnawing under the sink,
sleeps with a grey tabby cat, grown fat,
who came to her door, hungry.

Alone upstairs in her room
every night, she makes love
to her violin, frees the gypsy
songs of her youth from silver bonds.
Days, she attends funerals.

She's always first to the door of mourners,
bearing a casserole,
and of course, my father's bones,
carefully wrapped in her dream
of appearing at Carnegie Hall, and his,
of selling cartoons to The New Yorker.

Meanwhile, downstairs
in the yellow house,
where only she can place him,
my father still sits
in his green mohair chair
prickly as a barberry shrub
rooted in the faded rug.

Rich as tobacco smoke from his pipe,
her nocturnal serenade
rises from her violin's wooden throat
and floats from the open window,
calling down to him night after night,
a song only she can hear.

MONARCH

Your death on my lawn
appears to have been without trauma—
no bruises or fractures, no rips
in your orange velvet wings.
Even your black antennae
still sweep gracefully out—
mascaraed lashes. You are Cleopatra
gowned in mandarin satin, perfectly groomed,
reclining, your robe in regal folds.

Last autumn, I found
a migrating warbler,
victim of the plate glass kitchen window,
dead of a broken neck,
its eyes still reflecting sky.

Aztec blue, burnished bronze,
its body a feathered mystery
I could not solve. I buried it
in my garden, miles away
from its intended destination.

You, I recognize. But I don't know
the protocol for royal disposal.

I want to fly on your wings,
follow your veins'
intricate map to Mexican sun,
warm my skin on terra cotta cliffs—

For a month
I let your body rest
on the kitchen window sill.

Finally, frost builds in the trees
an amber kingdom of leaves, brilliant
as your wings, and I know I must

give you back to the sun,
toss you high
to catch the wind,
let you go—

flickering, fluttering,
spiraling, drifting, down
into the gold-leaf realm
you came from. And I understand

it isn't your beauty, but your freedom
I covet for my own.

IV

EXPOSING THE NEGATIVE

I

Holding a moss-colored suitcase
packed with memories of her mother,
my mother waits to board a jet,
fly alone to Switzerland,
meet cousins she's never seen.

At this moment she is a child
holding a camera focused
inward upon herself: "Smile."

My sister stands beside her.
I set the timer, then jump
into place beside them.

II

Each positive proof
reverses to negative,
faces vanish
from a tarnished mirror.

My daughter's image
is not on this film;
her own daughter
does not appear.

III

No mirror I own
permits me to see
into both my eyes at once.

IV

A summer night, shadows
eclipse other shadows.
My granddaughter's hand reaches out,
meets mine in a shining circle
not visible in mirror or lens.

Mothers, daughters, granddaughters,
an endless parade of silhouettes
cut from folded paper.
We are bonded hand to hand,
our faces a chain of blank white moons.

VI

In two weeks' time
Mother will kiss her cousins goodbye.
In her camera she'll carry
their images home:
wrinkled faces, ample bosoms,
stout legs rooted in sensible shoes.
Laughing like school girls,
they all will share
their paper embrace forever.

VII

Alone in the sky tonight,
Mother moves away from us all.
Out there with the stars she rides
her channel of light to the past,
even as the old moon rocks
the new moon sleeping
in her shining cradle.

RASPBERRY GATHERING

Blood runs its red current
between us, we know
what we know without saying.
Each of us keeps her own secrets,
seeds in a silent red cell.

My sister will never admit
to a lover, nor will I discuss
my husband's other woman,
and our mother won't even try to explain
what became of her father,
who disappeared
when she was twelve.

Today, we'd rather pick raspberries,
and so the three of us go
to the raspberry farm,
where children run in sun and wind
just as we once did,
climbing the hill behind our house
where raspberries grew wild.
We filled tin pans, filled our mouths,
laughed when juice ran down our chins—

Now, another summer's ripe
raspberries fall, all afternoon,
into our hands, and finally, we taste
our warm fruit, clustered together
at a wooden table, touching
each other's fingers,
eating berries from one basket.
After decades of pulling
apart, we're together—
mis-shapen fruit, but whole.

I do not need to ask the others
if they feel as ripe in the sun as I;
if they taste the richness
in this moment; if they sense
our final folding in of petals
before the blossom drops.

CELEBRATING HER 80TH

Marigolds, champagne,
chocolate cake on a tipsy card table
in the backyard; my mother,
sister and I decide
Mother must have a birthday ride
on the new carousel in the park.

We rotate slowly,
a three-star constellation—
round and round,
up and down, taking turns
smiling for each others' cameras,
our eyes bright as mica catching light.

Spinning in uneven orbit,
our faces soften,
grow round and smooth
as those of the children we circle,
faster and faster, passing
in a hurdy-gurdy whirling,
spangled as the fanciful
glass-eyed animals we ride.

It's hot. We're sweating.
Mother's wig slides to one side,
my sister's hair and mine frizzes
in the wind like clowns,
and our horses' eyes shine in the flash
with the same sudden candling
as those of wild animals
caught in headlights' glare,
marigolds exploding
inside our eyes.

GERANIUMS

On Mother's Day,
Mother sits with her leg
propped on a folding aluminum chair,
watching me plant geraniums
beside my father's grave.
I am trying not to notice
how she drags her own death
along with us.

Digging, I'm sweating; she shivers,
draws her jacket closer.
Rotten as an old stump, her leg purples,
sloughing off scab after scab
thick as bark. Beneath, pale skin shows
new growth. Another season, after all.

In autumn, we'll pull the geraniums up.
She'll roll them in newspaper
to winter them over;
I'll turn on the gro-light in my basement.

Blue as a star,
in spring it will whisper
of summer nights, bees, humidity.
The geraniums will green again,
their peppery fragrance rising.

I feel my fingers reaching deep
into earth, ancestry and love,
curling like tendrils under the ground,
urging new flowers to bloom
on what both of us know will become
her grave, and my own.

THE GIFT

"Hope is the hardest love we carry."
— Jane Hirshfield

In my mother's attic
my childhood waits,

a birthday present,
hidden in cardboard and tissue,
bound with cord no knife can cut.

Over and over
we unwrap the same package,
over and over

we offer each other
scoops of vanilla memory
melting on china plates.

Our party game
is always the same:
a smile for the camera.

The prize:
a brittle bouquet of old photos,
yellow and curled as spun-sugar roses.

In a brown paper bag
I bring mine home,
the souvenirs that prove

she tried to be my mother,
I tried to be her child.

SILENT MOVIE

In black and white memory,
my father appears
beside an open window,
his drawing board floating
in midnight florescence
awash in blue shadows,
white paper, black ink, silence.
Pen in one hand, cigarette in the other,
he sketches toward dawn—

I watch a film
spliced, edited by desire
to connect with a person, a place
impossible to revisit—

Beyond the lace of the maple tree
the streetlight does not illuminate
our lives behind curtains,
the closed eyes of sleepers,
the slow pulse of the mantel clock—

When the film runs out
my father remains
in the darkness that follows,
where he cannot age, die,
or cast a shadow on a screen
blank as a window in an empty house.

HOMECOMING

Don't go there. The rooms hold only shadows and dust.
There are no windows open to the scent of rain,

no dandelion bouquets or peanut butter sandwiches.
no hand-knit mittens, no chiming clock.

A sign says "Keep Out." Mother's alarm system
stands ready to intercept all trespassers, but

if you make it past the spiders in the basement
you'll find my father's heart and her father's ghost;

a jumble of jigsaw puzzles, many pieces missing;
two small girls, their hair in braids, and a pony.

You won't find the key to the attic, not even
a photograph album. No regrets or apologies,

no boxes of letters or handwritten journals,
no unmade beds, no dirty dishes in the sink.

Don't knock at the bolted door. The pony is gone.
An old woman with wind in her hair has ridden it away.

THERE'S THIS ABOUT LOSS

It makes you wish
you'd been born into a muslin body
with nothing inside except stuffing,
sawdust for brains, and a heart

painted on your chest
proclaiming "I love you"
to anyone who unbuttons your blouse.

You think it's a broken heart? I doubt it.
I've dealt mine out
so many times, it's thin
as a sliver of foil. I live

in a body fragile as a cracked egg.
My brain is a crossword puzzle:
more blanks than words.

The "I love you"
on my patchwork heart
is scarred into graffiti
I can't read or interpret, yet

it still beats steady,
bloody and alive
as the body of a woman
wheeled away after stillbirth.

And I can tell you this about loss:
The heart is the place it starts.

A GARDENER'S GUIDE TO THE COSMOS

Consider the roots
of frozen begonias,
how they cling—

the red stain
from melted petals
trickles down, bleeding
into my white garden gloves—

As I tug, I think
death may not come so easily
after all; blackness
may not work its way
into my heart, as it withers
a flower in frost;
my last image
may not be stars.

Yet I long to belong
to the dust of the universe.
Like a stone
dislodged and tumbling
into a desert canyon,

I am patient.
I have no roots,
only distance
beyond measure to travel.

MOON SHINING THROUGH TREES

Light wakens me, and I rise,
follow its path across the floor
where you and I made love one summer night,
the house only partially built.

Since then: Bricks. Glass. Doors. Locks. Death.
Tonight, moonlight slides over me,
silk over skin. Your hands on my breasts.
Under the flowering plum,

ripe fruit falls onto grass. The scent of you.
Staring into milky light, I want
only to see your face, feel your hands

touch mine, lift me
beyond this room, beyond my body,
beyond the point where branches enter sky.

THE CLEARING

Even where nothing is,
something is. Memory
drifts with blowing snow
over a red barn's roof

in the glass dome I hold
in my hand. There is a clearing,
and there I am with you
at the end of a road, stumbling

into snowdrifts. Laughing,
we fall, turn ourselves into angels,
our breath from their mouths
disappearing when we rise.

If I could, I would go with you
to that field, scatter your ashes
where your breath still floats,
frozen with mine, in clear cold air.

TREE HOUSE

I

In the old woods, the old house crumbles.
Walls fall down all around me.
I breathe the breath of raw earth,
fragrance of wet leaves.

In the new woods, I walk
where my bedroom will be, lie down
where I will sleep
on sheets of wild flowers,
violets and ferns.

I hold blue prints rolled in my hands,
my feet are wet and muddy.

II

Carpenters crawl like ants
over and under beams and boards.
Slowly, yellow and pine-scented,
a wooden tulip blooms.
The sky is still my roof.
The wound in my heart heals slowly.

III

Beside my front door
I plant a young pine,
not yet quite my own height,
an offering to the fallen trees
sheltering me now.
Birds nest in its branches all summer,
in winter it wears a halo of stars.

Acknowledgements

Grateful acknowledgement is made to the following publications, in which these poems first appeared: *Arts Indiana* for "Evening In Paris", "Getting It All Together", "Wedding Ghost", and "Widow's Love Song"; *Crazyhorse* for "Moon Shining Through Trees" and "The Window"; *Earth's Daughters* for "Handing Down The Recipe", and "Monarch"; *The Flying Island* for "Casa Rural", "Celebrating Her 80th", "The Clearing", "The Clockmaker's Daughter", "A Gardener's Guide To The Cosmos", "Geraniums", "New Moon Rising", "Raspberry Gathering", "September", "Sky Harbor Landing", "Traveling With Dr. Death", "Tree House", and "Westbound"; *Indiannual* for "Night Watch" and "Train Town Blues"; *Indianapolis Woman* for "Silk" and "Souvenir"; *Literally* for "Cooking With A Cuban Jazz Drum Solo"; *NUVO* for "On The Night Highway", and *Poetry-On-The-Buses* for "Apron Strings", and "The Robin's Egg." In addition, I would like to thank Always A River, Inc. for including "White Wake" in the anthology *Down The River*.

Special thanks to The Ragdale Foundation, for a residency during which the structure of this collection took shape.

My heartfelt thanks to Roger Mitchell, David Wojahn, and Maura Stanton. Their patience, wisdom, advice, support and thoughtful criticism has been invaluable to me.

To the members of my writing group, my fellow travelers on this mysterious road linking language and imagery, thank you all for making the journey with me: Alice Friman, Elizabeth Krajeck, Karen Kovacik, Bonnie Maurer, Catherine Swanson, and Elizabeth Weber. Your encouragement kept me moving forward.

And to Tony Gorsline and the staff at Cloudbank Books, who have worked so patiently on this book, thank you all for making it possible for *Night Highway* to appear on the map at last.

The daughter of an artist and a musician, Barbara Koons grew up in Mansfield, Ohio, where she began her writing career as a reporter and feature writer for the *Mansfield News-Journal*. She also has worked as a free-lance journalist, editor, and teacher. A non-traditional student, she earned her BA in English and MFA in Poetry at Indiana University after her children were grown.

An active volunteer with the Writers' Center of Indiana for nearly 20 years, she served as events co-ordinator and also as director of the Poetry In The Gallery reading series sponsored jointly with the Indianapolis Museum of Art.

Her poems have appeared in *Crazyhorse*, *Earth's Daughters*, *The Flying Island*, *The Hopewell Review* and other publications. She has received a number of awards for her poetry, including semi-finalist status in the "*Discovery*"/The Nation Competition in 2003. *Night Highway* is the first collection of her poems.